A PERIOD OF 4000 WEEKS

Embracing Time as Your Biggest Asset for a Fulfilling Existence

By

Ricky A. Bergman

COPYRIGHT © by Ricky A. Bergman 2024. All rights reserved.

No section of this book may be duplicated or transmitted in any form or by any means without authorization from the rightful owner of the copyright.

A Period of 4000 Weeks

CONTENTS

INTRODUCTION……………….4

THE SCIENCE AND PSYCHOLOGY OF TIME MANAGEMENT………………..8

STRATEGIES FOR PRIORITIZATION AND GOAL SETTINGS…………..16

TIME AND CALENDAR MANAGEMENT……………………22

OVERCOMING PROCRASTINATION AND TIME WASTERS……………………..29

WORK-LIFE BALANCE AND SELF-CARE………………….35

CONCLUSION…………………….41

ONE LAST THOUGHT…………….42

INTRODUCTION

The Time Management Myth: Dispelling Common Misconceptions

The common conception of time management is regularly misguided. Many individuals accept that time administration is all around, packing more assignments into their already-packed plans. Be that as it may, this mentality can lead to expanded stress, burnout, and a sense of never-ending busyness without really finishing what matters. In reality, time administration revolves around the amount of its approximate quality. It's around making mindful choices and prioritizing the activities that align with your objectives, values, and overall well-being. It's almost streamlining your needs and focusing on what matters.

A Period of 4000 Weeks

When you attempt to squeeze more assignments into your day without considering their significance, you'll discover yourself in a steady state of busyness, but not fundamentally fulfilling. Your time and vitality get spread lean across many exercises, taking off your feeling depleted and unfulfilled.

By streamlining your needs, you can distinguish the errands and exercises that have the most prominent effect on your individual and proficient life. This includes understanding your objectives, values, and long-term vision.

Once you have clarity on what matters to you, it becomes less demanding to designate your time and vitality accordingly. Effective time management requires making choices now and then saying no to tasks that do not align with your needs. It implies centering on high-value exercises that contribute to your general success and well-being. By doing so, you'll accomplish a sense of adjustment, efficiency, and fulfillment.

Brian Tracy, a famous creator and speaker on individual improvement and time administration, said,

> *"Time management is not about squeezing more tasks into your day; it's about simplifying your priorities and focusing on what truly matters."*

This quotation demonstrates the essence of effective time management, enabling you to adjust your perspective from quantity to quality.

A Period of 4000 Weeks

In the end, time management is about doing the right things, not about doing more. By detaching from your demands and focusing on the most important things, you can achieve greater efficiency, fulfillment, and a sense of reason.

1

THE SCIENCE AND PSYCHOLOGY OF TIME MANAGEMENT

"Time management is a reflection of self-management; the way we manage our time is a reflection of how we manage ourselves."

- Brian Tracy

The science and psychology of time management delve into the underlying principles and factors that influence your ability to effectively allocate and utilize your time. From a scientific perspective, research explores concepts such as cognitive load, decision-making processes, and the impact of external factors on your time management abilities. Understanding cognitive load helps you optimize decision-making while recognizing external influences that allow you to create environments conducive to productivity. Studies on psychological aspects like motivation, self-regulation, and procrastination help explain why people have trouble managing their time and offer solutions. Additionally, the psychology of time management explores the concept of flow, a state of deep engagement and focus, and its influence on time perception and productivity. By combining scientific findings and psychological principles, you can improve your time management skills and achieve a greater sense of control, productivity, and well-being in your lives. Understanding these three basic concepts can help you develop more personalized and sustainable time management strategies:

Cognitive load and decision-making

The idea of cognitive load, or the mental work needed to comprehend information and make judgments, is further explored in the science of time management. How you use your limited time and attention is greatly influenced by this.

When your cognitive load is high, you feel more mental stress, which can lead to poor decision-making, reduced productivity, and even decision fatigue. By understanding the dynamics of cognitive load, you can learn to organize your tasks and workflows in a way that minimizes unnecessary cognitive demands.

This can involve techniques such as grouping similar tasks, automating repetitive processes, or taking strategic breaks to refresh your mental resources. Managing cognitive load allows you to make more informed and effective decisions about how to prioritize your time and energy.

This establishes the groundwork for creating long-lasting, scientifically supported time management techniques that boost productivity and happiness.

Beyond Planning and Scheduling

Time management goes beyond simple planning and scheduling, it covers important aspects of implementation and review. While planning and scheduling are fundamental, effective time management requires implementing plans, adapting to unforeseen circumstances, and reviewing and evaluating your progress.

Execution includes carrying out planned tasks and activities. It requires discipline, focus, and the ability to prioritize effectively. Implementing strategies like the Eisenhower Matrix, which categorizes tasks based on their urgency and importance, can help you complete tasks systematically and efficiently.

Additionally, techniques like the Pomodoro technique, which involves working in focused bursts followed by short breaks, can improve your productivity during the performance phase.

Testing and evaluating your results are equally essential. Regular progress assessments allow for course corrections and ensure that your time is allocated to high-value activities.

This involves reflecting on your achievements, identifying areas for improvement, and making the necessary adjustments to your plans and schedules.

By reviewing your results and seeking feedback, you can refine your time management strategies and optimize your productivity.

Flow State and Time Perception

The concept of flow, introduced by psychologist *Mihály Csíkszentmihályi,* offers valuable insights for effective time management. Flow refers to a state of deep engagement and focused attention in which an individual is so immersed in an activity that time seems to pass quickly. When in a state of flow, people often report increased productivity, creativity, and a sense of satisfaction. This is because flow facilitates a cognitive state that minimizes distractions and allows for uninterrupted focus on the task at hand. By understanding the psychology of flow, you can learn to organize your tasks and environments in ways that encourage these optimal experiences.

This may involve tactics like dividing more complex work into digestible, skill-appropriate tasks, reducing outside disturbance, and striking the correct balance between knowledge and abilities.

Cultivating a flow state can lead to better time management as you will

A Period of 4000 Weeks

become more productive, focused, and intrinsically motivated in your work. In the end, this helps you maximize your limited time and attention while also improving your general health.

2

STRATEGIES FOR PRIORITIZATION AND GOAL SETTINGS

"The key is not to prioritize what's on your schedule, but to schedule your priorities."

- **Stephen R. Covey**

Effective prioritization and goal setting are essential skills to manage time and achieve desired results. Prioritization involves determining the relative importance and urgency of tasks and activities, while goal setting provides clear direction and purpose.

By implementing goal-setting and priority-setting strategies, you can optimize your time and resources, increase productivity, and strive to achieve your aspirations. Three interesting approaches to prioritization and goal setting are:

Setting SMART Goals

SMART goals are an effective strategy that provides a structured framework for goal-setting and increases the likelihood of success. **SMART** stands for **Specific, Measurable, Attainable, Relevant, and Time-bound**.

Specific goals are clearly defined and leave no room for ambiguity. They answer questions about what needs to be done, why it is important, and who is involved.

Measurable goals enable objective assessment of progress by incorporating quantitative criteria. It allows you to track your progress and stay motivated.

Achievable objectives are reasonable and doable. To ensure goals are reachable, they take into account the resources, abilities, and constraints that are accessible.

Relevant goals are consistent with broader aspirations, values, and priorities. They ensure emphasis and significant influence by being in line with entire goals, individual values, and strategic priorities.

Time-bound goals have a specific time frame or deadline, creating a sense of urgency and focus. They help you take responsibility and make progress over a period of time.

By adhering to SMART criteria, you can set clear, measurable, achievable, relevant, and time-bound goals.

Prioritization Matrix

Prioritization matrices, such as the Eisenhower matrix or the ABC analysis, are powerful tools for effectively managing time and resources. These matrices categorize tasks based on urgency and importance, providing a structured approach to prioritizing work.

The Eisenhower matrix, for instance, divides tasks into four quadrants: urgent and important, important but not urgent, urgent but not important, and not urgent and not important.

This framework enables you to quickly identify the tasks that require immediate attention, those that should be scheduled for later, and those that can be delegated or eliminated.

Similarly, the ABC analysis classifies tasks into three categories: A (high-priority, high-impact), B (medium-priority, medium-impact), and C (low-priority, low-impact).

By focusing your time and energy on A-tasks, you can ensure that the most essential activities receive the attention and resources they need.

These priority matrices enable you to make informed decisions about how to spend your limited time and energy, ultimately improving your overall productivity and efficiency.

Time Blocking

Time blocking is a time management technique that involves scheduling specific blocks of time for specific tasks or activities. By allocating specific time slots for different tasks, you can prioritize your activities in advance and structure your day.

This method helps manage competing priorities, minimize distractions, and ensure important tasks receive enough attention and focus.

Additionally, time blocking gives time allocation a visual representation, and facilitates the identification and correction of schedule imbalances and gaps. Breaking up your day into manageable chunks of time can help you increase productivity, stay focused, and complete your daily tasks effectively.

3

TIME AND CALENDAR MANAGEMENT

"Until you value yourself, you will not value your time. Until you value your time, you will not do anything with it."
— M. Scott Peck

Effective time and calendar management is a crucial part of overall productivity and well-being. This is a multi-layered approach that goes beyond simply planning events and meetings. This process involves the integration and synchronization of various calendars and planning tools.

By integrating personal, work, and shared calendars, you can get a complete overview of your commitments and avoid scheduling conflicts. Using calendar automation features like recurring events and automatic reminders makes time management even easier.

However, time and calendar management are not just about rigidity and structure. It also requires the ability to adapt to changing circumstances and maintain schedule flexibility. You can navigate the unpredictable nature of daily life by using the following approaches:

Time Tracking and Analysis

Time tracking and analysis is about monitoring the time spent on various tasks and activities to identify inefficiencies and improve productivity. Manual recording, automated software, and time tracking can be used.

A Period of 4000 Weeks

Evaluating the time and productivity lost is crucial. This means identifying procrastination plans, interruptions, distractions, and time wasted on low-priority work.

By analyzing time usage patterns and trends through reports and visualizations, you can understand when you are most productive, identify inefficient processes, and compare time usage over different periods.

This data approach enables informed decisions to optimize schedules, work habits, and time management strategies, ultimately leading to increased productivity and better time use.

Scheduling and Prioritization

This is an important aspect of time management and calendar management. There are various ways to plan your tasks and activities effectively. You can use daily, weekly, and monthly planners to define and assign specific periods for different activities.

Additionally, digital calendar apps give you the flexibility to schedule and update tasks on the go, set reminders, and share your calendar with colleagues and family members.

Managing conflicting priorities and multitasking is a challenge that people often face. Evaluating multitasking's viability and determining whether tasks can be completed concurrently without compromising quality is crucial. When priorities conflict, people may negotiate deadlines, delegate tasks, or seek help to complete them on time.

To avoid overscheduling and overbooking, you should consider your capacity and set realistic expectations. It is also prudent to leave buffer time between tasks to account for unexpected circumstances or to provide a mental break.

Collaboration and Coordination

Collaboration and coordination are essential for effective time and calendar management in team or collaborative settings. Sharing calendars and schedules with teams or colleagues allows for transparency and visibility of everyone's availability and commitments.

It enables you to efficiently plan meetings, tasks, and deadlines while considering the availability of team members. This practice fosters collaboration, avoids scheduling conflicts, and facilitates effective time allocation. Scheduling meetings and coordinating availability are crucial aspects of collaboration.

Calendar tools that offer features like availability sharing and auto-scheduling can simplify this process. By taking into account participants' availability and time zones, meetings can be scheduled to fit everyone's schedules, optimizing productivity.

Communicating schedule changes and updates promptly is crucial for maintaining coordination. Whether it's rescheduling a meeting or updating project timelines, you should promptly inform team members about any changes to ensure that everyone is aware of the updated schedules and can adjust their plans accordingly.

By implementing these practices, you and your team can work together cohesively, optimize time use, and achieve your shared goals.

4

OVERCOMING PROCRASTINATION AND TIME WASTERS

"Time wasted is time lost forever. Embrace discipline and take control of your actions to overcome procrastination." - John C. Maxwell

Overcoming procrastination and wasting time requires several strategies. Breaking large projects into smaller, manageable tasks and setting deadlines can help combat procrastination. It can also be motivating to reward yourself for progress. Effective time management techniques such as time blocking and prioritization can optimize productivity. It is extremely important to develop self-discipline and find inner motivation. Understanding the causes of procrastination and addressing the root causes can help overcome the problem.

By being mindful of wasted time and using technology and performance management tools, you can effectively manage your responsibilities.

Consistently applying these three tactics can help break unproductive habits and maximize productivity:

Identifying and Addressing Procrastination Triggers

To overcome this productivity-depleting habit, it's crucial to identify and address the causes of procrastination. Understanding root causes such as fear of failure, lack of interest, or poor time management can provide valuable insight into the underlying causes of procrastination. It is also important to recognize personal patterns and habits of procrastination. Once the causes and patterns have been identified, it's time to develop targeted strategies. Poor time management may require implementing a structured schedule, prioritizing tasks, and eliminating distractions. When there is no interest, find ways to make tasks fun or connect them to personal values to increase motivation. By understanding the unique causes and patterns of procrastination, you can adapt your approach and implement personalized strategies to effectively combat this behavior.

Effective Time Management Techniques

A Period of 4000 Weeks

Effective time management techniques can be a powerful tool to overcome procrastination and increase productivity. Time blocking involves allocating specific time slots for different tasks and activities to ensure focused work without distractions or wasted time. This method helps create a structured schedule and a sense of responsibility. Prioritization is another important aspect of time management.

By defining and ranking your tasks according to importance and deadline, you can ensure that the most critical and urgent tasks are completed first, thus avoiding the tendency to put off essential tasks. Setting realistic goals and deadlines can create a sense of urgency and motivation, encouraging you to complete tasks on time.

Clear goals and deadlines provide orientation, structure, and a sense of achievement and reduce the likelihood of procrastination. By consistently applying these time management techniques, you can develop better habits, concentrate better, and resist the temptation to procrastinate, ultimately leading to higher productivity and more efficient use of time.

Building Self-Discipline and Motivation

Developing self-discipline and motivation is crucial to overcoming procrastination. Creating a daily routine and sticking to it provides a sense of discipline and consistency.

The aim is to set specific work, break, and leisure times to ensure efficient time management. A well-structured daily routine reduces the temptation to procrastinate and helps you stay focused.

Seeking accountability through partnerships or support systems can also be effective. Sharing goals and progress with others creates a sense of accountability and encourages you to stay on track.

This can be achieved through regular check-ins, accountability friends, or joining groups with similar goals. Implementing these strategies requires commitment and consistency.

5

WORK-LIFE BALANCE AND SELF-CARE

"Self-care is not selfish. You cannot serve from an empty vessel."

- Eleanor Brownn

Work-life balance and self-care are crucial to maintaining a healthy and fulfilling lifestyle. By balancing work and private life, you can prioritize your well-being and prevent burnout. Self-care practices such as regular exercise, adequate rest, and activities that bring joy and relaxation contribute to overall physical and mental health.

Proactive time management, setting limits, and prioritizing self-care can lead to a successful work-life balance. This balance improves productivity, reduces stress, and promotes feelings of satisfaction. You are better prepared to excel in all aspects of life if you have a solid foundation of work-life balance and self-care. The following subtopics cover specific strategies and techniques for achieving a healthy work-life balance:

Prioritizing Self-Care Practices

Priorltizing self-care routines is essential for maintaining a healthy work-life balance and overall well-being. This involves devoting time and effort to various self-care tasks. Physical activity and healthy food habits improve physical well-being, increase vitality, and decrease push. Consolidating typical fitness routines can have a positive impact on your overall health and wellness.

Stress-management procedures like reflection, yoga, and profound breathing workouts give you mental restoration and help oversee stretch levels.

Getting enough rest is critical for your optimal performance and efficiency. Creating a consistent rest plan and a relaxing sleep pattern will help you sleep better for mental recovery.

Prioritizing these self-care habits allows you to better manage stress, preserve physical and mental health, and live a more balanced and full life, resulting in increased productivity and happiness in both professional and personal domains.

Establishing Boundaries and Time Management

Setting boundaries and implementing effective time management strategies are crucial to maintaining work-life balance. Here are some key points to consider:

Setting realistic expectations and learning to say "no" are crucial to setting boundaries. By understanding personal boundaries and priorities, you can avoid overcommitting and prevent work from interfering with your time. Learning to decline requests that don't align with your personal goals or values can save you valuable time and energy.

It is critical to schedule time for personal and family affairs. Setting aside distinct time slots for things such as exercise, hobbies, family time, and self-care ensures that these elements of life receive the attention they need. This fosters a well-balanced and fulfilling existence.

Building a Supportive Environment

Creating a supportive workplace is essential for encouraging work-life balance and self-care. It is critical to foster open communication among colleagues, bosses, and family members. Creating an environment in which you feel comfortable addressing your concerns, needs, and desires makes it simpler to identify solutions that promote work-life balance.

Open communication promotes understanding, empathy, and collaboration to establish tactics that benefit everyone involved. Seeking guidance from mentors, coaches, or employee assistance programs can be quite beneficial. These resources offer tips, ideas, and tools for achieving work-life balance and self-care. Developing a positive work culture that encourages work-life balance is beneficial to your well-being.

You can develop open communication, seek support from mentors or assistance programs, build a positive work culture, and implement well-being initiatives to create a friendly atmosphere that fosters work-life balance and self-care.

CONCLUSION

To ensure long-term management success, prioritize flexibility and adaptation in your time management strategy. Flexibility and adaptation are essential in the ever-changing management world. Effective time management entails more than simply keeping to a schedule.

Adapting to change is crucial for long-term success. You can overcome problems, make educated decisions, and achieve long-term success in a dynamic and ever-changing corporate environment.

ONE LAST THOUGHT

"Life is not measured by the number of breaths we take, but by the moments that take our breath away."

- Maya Angelou

The sands of time have moved in 4,000 weeks, and new chapters in your life have begun. In the final pages, reflect on your adventure. Moments of victory, lessons learned, shared, and dreams accomplished.

With this concluding idea, remember that life is measured not only by ticktocks but also by the breadth of your experiences and the connections you make. It serves as a reminder to appreciate the last week, to live in the present now, and to embrace the beauty of change.

A Period of 4000 Weeks

Did you experience a change in perspective on time management after reading *A Period of 4000 Weeks*? I hope so!

Please consider leaving a review on Amazon through the QR code below to help us reach more readers and continue creating valuable content. Your feedback will make a real difference.

Thank you for your support!

www.ingramcontent.com/pod-product-compliance
Lightning Source LLC
Chambersburg PA
CBHW070952220526
45471CB00007B/2994